A Weymouth Story

2

A Weymouth Story

2

Independence Is Won; A Nation Is Born

By

Lawrence G. Lambros

iUniverse, Inc.

New York Bloomington

A Weymouth Story 2

iUniverse books may be ordered through booksellers or by contacting:

iUniverse
1663 Liberty Drive
Bloomington, IN 47403
www.iuniverse.com
1-800-Authors (1-800-288-4677)

ISBN: 9781440156038 (pbk)
ISBN: 9781440156045 (ebk)

Printed in the United States of America

iUniverse rev. date: 7/29/2009

Introduction

This is a story written in two parts: *Time, Indians, Settlers, and Townships* and *Independence Is Won; A Nation Is Born.*

This book tells the story of the American Revolution and the role Weymouth's citizens played in that war, which set the stage for the birth of our nation, the United States of America. It is the story of how Weymouth citizens lived during that period of our history. It is a story about the Declaration of Independence and the Constitution of the United States, which established the laws that give us the rights and freedoms we enjoy today. The story ends with a helicopter ride over Weymouth to view its numerous historical buildings and sites.

This is not a history book. It is an effort to bring history alive, as if you were there with those people and in those places when it happened. Although places and dates are accurate, some names are fictitious.

Acknowledgments

I thank Theodore G. Clarke, member of the Weymouth Historical Society and Chairperson of the Weymouth Historical Commission, for his support and knowledgeable contributions in editing the historical content of the story.

My thanks go to Michele Pomarico Hamilton and Natalie Pomarico Lambros for serving as first-draft editors and for their valuable suggestions to help the story read smoothly.

I also thank Christopher Hannon, PhD, Thomas Curtis, Stephen Ford, James Cunningham, and Robert Luongo for their early support of the project.

Special thanks go to the Teaching American History Grant Director, John DeCoste, and Assistant Directors Patricia Cronin and John Magner Jr., for supporting and recommending the funding of this project.

The following resources were used in creating this story: the four-volume *History of Weymouth* by George Walter Chamberlain and the Weymouth Historical Society; Theodore G. Clarke's *History of Weymouth, My First History Book: Learning about Weymouth* by Elaine Dwyer and Kathy Pijewski; and *The Encyclopedia of American History* by Richard B. Morris.

1

Larry made a remarkable discovery in the History Resource Room of the local library. He found a computer and a monitor there that everyone thought were damaged. There was no connecting cable, nor was there an electric cord with a plug. That first day, when he turned the computer and the monitor around to look at them more carefully, he accidentally touched the screen, and a word puzzle appeared that seemed to suggest a number of historical events. He touched the screen again, and the words *Time, Indians, Settlers, and Townships* appeared, and the computer began to show and tell a story about the beginning of our solar system. The computer voice narrated the story, while the monitor displayed an amazing sequence of scenes explaining the Big Bang theory, gravitational forces in space, and the beginnings of our solar system and our planet Earth. Larry and his best friend, Tom, watched as the Earth changed from boiling hot volcanic lava to the planet we know today.

When the computer and monitor were put away in the library cellar with the other damaged furniture, Larry and Tom had to sneak into the cellar storage area to continue their adventure.

They asked Mrs. Hamilton, the librarian, if they could take the computer and monitor home to repair them. Mrs. Hamilton made the arrangements and asked the boys to promise that, if and when they did fix the computer, they would return it to the library.

The boys spent late afternoons and Saturdays in the secrecy of Larry's cellar playroom for the four next weeks, listening, watching, and learning. They watched and learned about the Earth, its early inhabitants, the Indians, and the coming of the white man from Europe. They watched and learned about the settlements in Jamestown, Plymouth, Charlestown, Boston, Hingham, and Weymouth. They learned what life was like for those earliest settlers. They watched families move from one busy community to another, and then, slowly, out into the wilderness of nearby, unsettled lands. They listened and watched as a new generation began to resist taxes levied upon them and laws imposed upon them by the king's appointees to the Great and General Court in Boston.

The boys watched as the settlers in Weymouth struggled to establish their farms and their businesses and build a church and a school.

"Larry, what mark did you get on your project?" asked Tom.

"I got an A. What did you think I would get? I had no trouble writing my paper after listening to and watching this computer and monitor the last few weeks. This thing is like a private tutor. I hope it still works! Where were we when we left off?" asked Larry as he moved toward the computer and the monitor sitting on the table at the far end of the playroom in his cellar. "Well, let's see," he said as he touched the monitor's screen and waited anxiously to see whether history would visit them again. *Independence Is Won; A Nation Is Born* were among the numerous words and phrases lit up on the screen. "I think that's what comes next," explained Larry, as he touched the words on the screen. The screen lit up.

"Look at that picture," pointed Tom as the monitor showed farmer John Pratt walking down Summer Street toward Weymouth Landing and the wharf on the Fore River. On the way, he met old Sam Bates. The boys watched and listened.

"Where are you headed?" asked Sam.

"I'm going down to the wharf and then over to the general store. Has the ship from Boston come in yet?"

"I reckon so. I've seen lots of folks on Front and Commercial Streets today. Most of them seem to be headed for the docks."

Aaron Reade joined them.

"I'll be shearing my sheep soon. What's this I hear about you growing a field of flax at your place, Sam?" asked Aaron.

"Well, I've heard that you can spin flax and weave it into fine cloth just the way they do with spun cotton and sheep's wool. They call it linen. A lot of the city folks wear fancy linen clothes nowadays. We aren't getting many clothes from England anymore, or as much cotton from the South, either. Everyone can't wear wool, you know! It's too hot most of the time and too itchy all of the time!" complained Sam. "So, I'm going to try to make some linen for the Missus."

"I'll stick with my sheep and my woollies," replied Aaron. "I hope the linen works out well for you, Sam. I've got to get going. I want to be back in time for that warm rye and Injun bread that the little lady makes every Friday."

The picture on the monitor changed and showed Aaron leading his sheep over to Cranberry Pond.

One of Aaron's sons complained, "Why do we have to wash and scrub the sheep, Papa?"

"We're cleaning these animals so that their wool will be as clean as possible when we shear them. Spring is here and shearing time has come."

"Am I big enough to help you shear?"

"If your mother says that you're big enough to help scrub, then I reckon you're big enough to help shear. Here, let me show you how to do this," explained Aaron. "You can use these shears. Be very careful. They're very sharp. I just edged them on the stone wheel yesterday. Watch. You try to cut the wool so that you can cut off one big piece, if possible. Don't worry, she won't move. She knows what you're doing. She's glad to get that heavy coat off her back. She's getting mighty hot herself by this time of the year. See, like this, all one piece, in one careful cut right off her back. We call this a fleece. It didn't hurt her a bit. Now you try it. Careful, be careful! Good job, son, good job."

The boys watched Aaron and his son bring the sheep and the fleece back to the barn and then go into the house.

"Mother and the girls will comb out the fleece into stringy strands of wool. Then they will take the strands of wool off the comb and spin them together on the spinning wheel and make long strings of soft thread called yarn. They'll dye the yarn with berry juice and weave it into woolen cloth on the loom over there," explained Aaron.

"Then they'll make sweaters, caps, pants, and underwear!" laughed his youngest son. "I hate itchy woolen long johns!"

Larry touched the screen, and the picture faded.

"Life was sure tough for those early settlers. They planted and grew all their own food. They made most of their own clothes and worked six long days a week. Seems like they spent all day Sunday in church," said Larry.

"I didn't know that most girls didn't go to school back then. I guess the girls had to work around the house all the time. They worked in the fields, made clothes, and took care of the babies. Those early settlers sure had lots of kids," observed Tom.

"They needed a lot of kids to help on the farm to do all the work. My teacher told me that a lot of the kids died when they were babies or when they were young. There was no aspirin or other miracle medicines back then. Sometimes, even the mother died when she had a baby. So, families had lots of kids to help do all the work. Well, it's time for you to go home. See you tomorrow after school," said Larry.

2

The boys met in Larry's playroom the next afternoon after school. When Larry put the computer and monitor on, the picture took them inside one of the homes in Weymouth. The computer voice spoke: "The sheep were sheared, the woolen yarn was spun, and the cloth woven and dyed. Spring became summer. The gardens were dug, the stones and rocks were removed, and the seeds were planted. The spring and summer rains came. Later that summer, the vegetables and the fruit were picked. The cutting and storing of hay and the sight of the low, orange moon meant that the time for the last harvest had come, and plans for winter had to begin."

"Stephen, will Englebury be home for Thanksgiving?" asked Mrs. Saunders.

"I really don't know. He's down off the Cape, fishing. You know that he loves the sea. I hope he'll make it home for Thanksgiving. I hear that Mr. Tufts has a ship moored on the Fore River and that the Humphreys have one anchored in the harbor. There was a day when we were all farmers. Now, many of our sons are becoming shop owners, cobblers, lumber mill workers, boatbuilders, blacksmiths, and fishermen," replied Stephen.

"Well, you can't expect all the boys to be farmers. Working this rocky soil is mighty hard work. I don't blame some of the youngsters for turning to the sea and other vocations. The fishing industry is very important. We're sending our salted cod all the way to Europe these days. Fishing is a big business. I just hope Englebury is safe."

"Mother, we've got to get ready for winter. All the apples and pears are in the barn," reported Stephen.

"Yes, I know. I've already started preserving the fruits. We'll have grape preserves this year, too," said Mrs. Saunders.

"How about the vegetables—are they done?"

"Now Stephen, you just worry about the meat, and I'll take care of the vegetables like I always do! The squash and turnips are done. So are the beans and tomatoes. I'll do the pumpkin after the last hay harvest, just like I always do. Don't get nervous. We'll have plenty to eat this winter. Is Old Man Bates going to help you slaughter the hogs?"

The boys watched as Mrs. Saunders got up from the table and put a loaf of corn bread into the built-in oven in the fireplace.

"I love your warm corn bread, Mother," said Stephen.

"Don't forget that you've got to bring a load of corn over to Able's gristmill. He's so busy, you won't get it for a week. I want the cornmeal in small bags this time. Those big bags are getting too heavy for me," ordered Mrs. Saunders as Stephen disappeared through the door and into the evening twilight.

Larry pulled his chair up closer to the monitor as he watched Stephen go around the corner toward the barn and call back over his shoulder, "I'll see David at meeting tonight. I expect he'll help me butcher the hog. If not him, someone will."

The boys watched Stephen feed the chickens, ducks, and hogs.

The computer voice spoke. "The Saunders didn't raise sheep. They bought their woven woolen cloth from the general store and made their own clothes, but they did raise hogs. Stephen Saunders butchered his hogs and sold the meat to his neighbors who didn't have hogs and to the merchants who came down from Boston to meet him at the docks especially to buy his smoked hams and bacon."

The monitor showed Stephen walking back into the house. He said, "This year, I'm going to bring the hide over to the new tannery and have it tanned. We'll have that traveling cobbler make us some new shoes if he comes by this year."

"Why are the men having a meeting in the middle of the week?" Mrs. Saunders asked.

"There's quite a bit of talk about the king and his taxes."

"Now, you stay clear of politics, Stephen Saunders. I don't want all that arguing and fussing going on in my front room all winter long!"

"Now, dear, don't be talking so loud. You don't want anyone to think that I'm not the master of my own home," laughed Stephen as he headed for the woodpile. Then he mumbled under his breath to himself, "These women will want to vote next!"

"What did you say?" asked Mrs. Saunders.

"Your ears are too good," answered Stephen.

Next, Larry and Tom saw a picture of the Saunders's backyard. Stephen Saunders and Mr. Bates were butchering three big hogs. One of the neighbor's children was standing by. He was crying.

"Son, we've got to eat this winter. This hog is where we get most of our meat for the winter, and the meat from those hogs over there will be shipped to Boston so that we can sell it and earn enough money to keep the farm going. Those are the facts of life, young man. Where do you think your Papa gets those rabbits and turkeys for Sunday dinner? He shoots them!"

The young boy ran off toward his home, crying.

"Must be the first time he's seen an animal butchered," reflected Mr. Bates.

Larry went upstairs to get a couple glasses of soda. When he returned, he and Tom heard Mrs. Saunders yell out from the kitchen window, "Don't forget to cut the shoulder meat into long strips, Stephen. I'll jerk and smoke them tomorrow. Remember, you said you liked it that way last year."

"Are you going to butcher your steer this year, David?"

"Don't know. It probably depends on how many deer and rabbit I shoot by the end of the month. I'd like him to grow a little bigger before I cut him up."

The boys watched the men skin the hogs, cut the bodies into pieces of meat, and hang them over a smoky fire in the back of the barn. Later, they watched Mrs. Saunders come out of the house and take some of the pieces of meat and put them into a barrel.

She said, "I'll let these marinate and soak a few weeks longer this year than last. They'll stay preserved longer, and they'll taste better, too!"

Tom commented, "People really had to work hard in those days. No supermarkets for them!"

Stephen Saunders shared with David Bates, "If and when you slaughter that steer of yours, I'll trade you some of our salt pork for some of your beef. I'll even help you butcher him."

The computer voice explained, "In the early 1700s, families in Weymouth hunted and ate rabbit, deer, turkey, pheasants, and quail. They raised their own chickens, roosters, pigs, hogs, sheep, cows, and cattle. Men and boys hunted squirrel and fox. They used the hides of the animals they hunted and butchered to make leather shoes, hats, saddles, and jackets. They used the fur to make hats, mittens, coats, and shoe linings. Many of the men in the northern end of Weymouth had their own fishing boats. People ate smoked and cured meat, fresh and salted fish, and fresh clams and lobsters. The extra fish was sold to the markets in Boston, and some was even sent across the sea to Europe."

The computer voice continued, "By Thanksgiving, families had stored or traded for their winter's supply of meat, including dried and salted fish. Vegetables and fruits were preserved. Bayberries and animal fats were used to make candles. Cow's milk and goat's milk were churned into butter and cheese. Soap was made from lye and animal fat. Food was stored for the winter in small stone houses built into the side of a hill near the house or in the cellar, if there was one. Men and boys cut wood, split logs, and piled them up next to the food storage house or in the barn. Everyone worked hard. They were ready for the long, cold winter."

The image on the monitor took Larry and Tom inside the Saunders home once again. The computer voice reported, "Englebury Saunders was lost at sea. His fishing boat broke up in a hurricane off the tip of Cape Cod."

Larry and Tom heard Stephen Saunders pray at the Thanksgiving meal, "We thank you for our blessings. We thank you for our freedom and our health. We thank you for this new land. We thank you for our son. We know thy will was done. We know that our son is with thee. We pray that you will watch over us all and protect this family each and every day. Amen."

Larry looked at Tom and said, "That's a sad story. A lot of fishermen were lost at sea in those days. There were no weathermen to predict hurricanes."

3

The next afternoon, after school, Larry and Tom watched the picture on the monitor, which showed families walking and riding to the new church in South Weymouth.

The computer voice explained, "In 1723, the settlers in the southern part of Weymouth asked the Great and General Court in Boston to allow them to become the Second Precinct of Weymouth. John Torrey was sent to the court to argue against the separation. The people in the northern part of town didn't want the town split into two precincts. The court in Boston decided in South Weymouth's favor. They built their own church in the South Village, which today is called Columbian Square."

The picture on the monitor changed back to North Weymouth and showed the Hunt family getting ready to go to church. The computer reported, "The First Church, on Church Street, had burned down the year before, in 1751. It was the second church on that site. The first one was built back in 1680. The people of North Weymouth attended church in a temporary meetinghouse on the site while plans for a new church were discussed."

The boys heard Mrs. Hunt say, "Come on, we'll be late for meeting."

"I'll be right there. I'm putting on my store-bought, Sunday-go-to-meeting coat. I think that tailor made it just a little too snug," complained Mr. Hunt.

"Too snug!" laughed Mrs. Hunt. "You're just getting too fat. I'm feeding you too well. Hurry along. The children and I will go ahead with the Lowells."

"Go ahead, then. I'll come along with Jonas. Where on earth are you, Jonas? There you are. Come on, son. Haven't you finished cleaning my boots yet?"

"Yes, sir, here they are, sir. They're as soft as new!"

"You know, Jonas, there is not one bit of difference between the right boot and the left boot. That traveling cobbler uses the same wooden last for both feet. He makes all his boots the same way. I can hardly wear them. My right foot is bigger than my left. Next time, I'm going to make my own leather boots! Come on Jonas, let s go to church. I think we are late."

Larry and Tom watched as Mr. Hunt and his son Jonas caught up with Mrs. Hunt, the other children, and the Lowells.

"Good morning to you, Charles. Good morning, Mrs. Lowell," said Mr. Hunt as he and Jonas approached the small group of people walking ahead to church.

"Hello, James. Good morning to you," replied Mr. Lowell. The men shook hands. "Good morning, Jonas," he added.

"Good morning, sir," responded Jonas with a bow.

The picture on the monitor showed the women walking ahead together in a group. The children ran, while the men walked at a slow pace, talking about the problems of the day.

"Well, Charles, what do you think about this freedom talk?"

"We've been a colony for quite a few years now, Jim. It's been over a hundred years. This is 1752. It's about time we began to think about a different relationship with the king and with England. But our immediate problem is to build a new meetinghouse after that horrible fire last year."

"You're right. Old Man Bates and John White have asked me to be on a committee with them to look into that. I think that we should build a new one soon. Reverend Smith has asked us to build pews for each family and charge a fee of ten pounds. That'll help pay for about half of the building. The men will donate their labor, of course. Then, we'll assess all the members for the other half of the cost. That way we'll not go into debt. What do you think?"

"Sounds like a right good idea to me," replied Mr. Lowell. "We also need to talk to Braintree about repairing and widening the cart bridge over the river down in the Landing. It is fifteen years old now and getting dangerous."

The computer reported, "Earlier in 1736, a wooden cart bridge had been built over the Monatiquot River where it runs into the Fore River in Weymouth Landing. It allowed people to travel from Boston through Quincy, Braintree, Weymouth, Abington, and all the way to Plymouth and back."

Larry and Tom watched families entering the temporary meetinghouse. The computer reported, "The service was a long one. The preacher often talked for two hours or more. As time went on, a few of the men went to sleep. The women and younger girls sat up straight on the wooden benches, seldom looking left or right and seldom moving a muscle. The boys squirmed and were uneasy sitting for such a long time. Most of the boys had run on the way to meeting and were sweaty and itchy in their woolen underwear. Jonas could not run. The left side of his body had been crippled by the palsy."

After the service, the monitor showed the women trading gossip on the lawn and the men trading stories and ideas on the front steps. Larry and Tom watched as some of the children played games and told each other stories about the schoolmaster. Boys chased girls, and girls giggled. Jonas watched.

The computer voice reported, "After the morning church service, if the weather permitted, families sat on the grass and ate a small box lunch. They went back into the meetinghouse for the two-hour afternoon service after lunch. Sunday was indeed the Lord's day."

The monitor took the boys inside the home of Reverend Smith. The computer voice added, "The men were talking once again about independence from England. Reverend Smith listened and thought of his daughter, Abigail, who was proving to be quite an independent girl herself.

"Abigail Smith had been born on November 23, 1744. Reverend Smith was the pastor of the First Church. Mrs. Smith was the daughter of the Quincy family, which lived in Braintree.

"Abigail was a slender girl. Her parents decided not to send her to a tutor but to educate her at home. Abigail was very smart, very curious, and learned quickly.

"When she was close to twenty, a young student from Harvard University named John Adams often visited her home to participate in tutorials with her learned father. Their home was a modern one for the times. It had glass windows, more than one fireplace, and a second floor as well.

"John Adams was very smart, and he and Abigail often discussed issues and studied together. They fell in love. In 1764, they were married. Abigail Smith Adams and John Adams moved into their new farmhouse in Braintree near Penn's Hill. Over the next few years, Abigail took over the running of the farm and property because John was a busy lawyer in Boston. He was seldom home. He became a very important political leader in Massachusetts. He served as an ambassador to France and England. He later served as the new nation's second president. Abigail wrote letters to him almost every day over the many months each year that he was away on legal and government business. One of her letters showed her longing for him to be home with her and her four children. It read, '... how many snowflakes divide thee and me ...'"

4

The boys listened as the computer voice continued, and the monitor showed the busy streets leading to the wharves in North Weymouth and the Landing. "During the 1760s, Weymouth was a busy place. Ships and boats came up the Fore River and Back River loaded with supplies from England and Boston. Ships came from other ports of Europe with fine furniture and new clothes. Some of the sea captains lived in the Landing near the river and near the wharves in North Weymouth. Many of the young men had left farming to sail the seas or work in the local shops or in Boston to make a better living."

The monitor pictured the busy shops, the saw mills, and the gristmills. The boys watched men working in the blacksmith shop and in the tannery.

The computer voice explained, "More of the women wore store-made clothes made of silk, linen, or cotton for Sunday meetings. Most men still wore gray suits of homemade woolen cloth. Ships carried large loads of logs and cut lumber and barrels of fish from Weymouth to Boston and across the ocean to England. Farmers cut down the forests and sold their logs to the city of Boston because they had already used up much of the forest in and around the city and nearby villages to build their many homes, meeting houses, and shops. Most of the logging was done in the western and southern sections of Weymouth, as land was cleared for dairy and vegetable farms along Summer Street, Front Street, and Pleasant Street. Ice houses were built on Whitman's Pond, Mill Pond, and Great Pond. Mill Pond no longer exists. Its dam is gone, and its small remaining stream runs down from Great Pond in South Weymouth through a large pipe under Front Street, the expressway, and under Middle Street as it empties into Whitman's Pond. Houses now sit where Mill Pond once existed. The lumber mill and the lumberyard are also gone."

"My grandfather used to swim in Mill Pond and play hockey there," exclaimed Tom. "Now it's gone."

The computer voice continued, "There were sawmills to cut wood and gristmills to grind corn and grain into meal and flour. There were carpenters who built and rebuilt houses, barns, and sheds. Boatbuilders were busy throughout the year, and the tannery made leather out of

13

all kinds of hides. Most of the homes had glass windows, and many had black, iron, wood-burning stoves. There were grandfathers and grandmothers and lots of little grandchildren. There were close to 1500 people living in Weymouth by the mid-1700s. New families brought new ideas. Colonial leaders in Boston and the surrounding towns were talking again about property rights, taxes, freedoms and the king.

New roads were cut through the woods and across pastures to help people travel from the North Village to the Landing and from the Landing to the southern end of the town. Weymouth was a large town. Roads were built from the East Village and the Herring Run to a busy nearby Hingham harbor. The dirt roads were hard to travel and were rutted by the wagons that traveled them daily. Wagonbuilders, wheelmakers, leatherworkers, and blacksmiths, who made horseshoes and tools out of iron, were busy in their barns and in the new shops. The main roads in the center of the four villages of the town were lined with new houses and shops. Many of those old dirt roads were Indian paths that became the roads we use today to travel around our town and between the towns of the South Shore. More cemeteries were created. The town was getting older. The older generation was dying, and a new generation was taking its place."

Tom spoke out as the monitor depicted what looked like a battle between French soldiers in blue uniforms and well-dressed English soldiers in red coats who were supported by a group of mostly bearded mountain men on horseback. The battle was taking place along a riverbank in the deep forest, just outside a high wooden stockade at a fort with a French flag waving above it.

"I think that's the beginning of the French and Indian War."

"Shh, listen to the computer," urged Larry.

The computer reported, "In 1754, a group of colonial volunteers from Delaware, Virginia, and the Carolinas marched into the Ohio Valley with English army regulars to recapture the English forts there that had been taken earlier by the French army from Canada. The English General Braddock was killed. George Washington, a Virginian volunteer, lost two horses from under him but survived the campaign. The combined troops of English redcoats and colonial volunteers drove the French out of the Ohio Valley and back into Canada."

Then the picture on the monitor showed the inside of the poorly-lit Arnold Tavern in Weymouth Landing. "Sailors from the ships that docked at the wharf on the Fore River often came there and drank ale and related their sea stories."

The boys continued to listen to the computer, as they saw Mr. Trufant stride into the noisy tavern and cry, "Did you hear the news?"

"What news?" asked Nathan Ames.

Mr. Trufant glanced over toward a French sailor who was standing at the bar and said, "If I were you, Frenchy, I'd get on my ship in a hurry and get out of here. I think there is going to be trouble around here soon."

"Why?" asked Caleb Joy, who was standing by listening.

"Well, I've heard that the French and English are fighting up at Lake George. The word is that French troops had moved down from Canada into the Ohio Valley and taken over the English outposts there. Braddock and Washington recaptured the forts and ran them off. Braddock was killed. Now it looks like the French will try to come down into New England and claim the lands south of the Saint Lawrence."

The men at the table looked at the French sailor. One of the local sailors explained, "Now, we're not going to hang this French merchantman, this sailor, just because he's French, are we? It's not his fault that the Frenchies in Canada are getting ready to make a big mistake! He's a seaman, just like the rest of us." He continued, as he glanced toward the French sailor, "We mean you no harm."

"I'll drink to that!" laughed one of the bystanders.

The boys watched the men sitting and standing around the table slap the French sailor on the back, laugh, and raise their mugs.

"Tell us, Joseph," Cotton Tufts said. "How'd all this trouble begin?"

"Maybe our French friend here can tell us," said Ebenezer with a smile, as he put his hand on the Frenchman's shoulder.

"You know, I really don't understand," said the French sailor. "I suppose it is a fight for the land, yes? Our king thinks he owns the New World. Your king thinks that he owns the New World, and the king of Spain thinks he owns the New World. It seems to me that there should be enough room for everyone, eh?"

"That's one good thing about the sea," spoke out one of the seamen at the table. "There's room for everyone on the sea—most of the time." They all laughed again and raised their mugs in agreement.

"Yes, but they are fighting over control of the sea, too," lamented the bartender.

The boys watched as the tavern quieted to a whisper, and Mr. Trufant spoke. "There's more news. Ben Lincoln has called for volunteers to join the king's army. It seems as though the Indians to the north have joined up with the French and are winning the battle at Lake George up there. The governor has asked towns to send volunteers to help the king's regulars squash the French incursion and drive the French back into Canada. Volunteers will move out the day after tomorrow. We are expected to reach Fort Henry in a week or so and make a stand there."

"I'll volunteer!" cried Solomon Lovell.

"You can count on me!" exclaimed another.

"No one should volunteer now. Wait until morning, when the drink has worn off. Then make up your minds," recommended Samuel Thaxter.

Larry and Tom noticed the French sailor slip quietly out the side door of the tavern.

Next, the monitor showed a group of young men in front of the meetinghouse. Most of them were volunteering to march north with the men from Hingham and Cohasset to help the English troops repel the French and Indian attackers. The picture changed. The boys watched as a French ship sailed down the Fore River and out toward the bay.

The computer voice reported, "A small number of young volunteers marched out of Weymouth to meet up with the volunteers from Scituate, Cohasset, Hingham, and Braintree to march north. A few weeks later, a tired and worn-out company of volunteers returned."

The monitor showed women and children crying with joy to see their husbands, sons, and brothers return home safely. "Did you whip those French Papists?" shouted one old-timer.

Officer Trufant spoke with his head bowed. "We got there too late. The French and Indians had wiped out the English regulars at Fort William Henry. Some of the regulars were scalped! We had to turn back. We had no orders, and we were without a plan."

"Best you did, you saved our boys," said one mother thankfully.

"We're going back," shouted one of the volunteers. "We'll march again. This time we'll drive them all the way back up to Canada where they belong!"

Larry and Tom watched as the company of volunteers and the younger boys, still too young to go off to war, applauded with excitement.

As the picture on the monitor faded, the computer voice observed, "Later that year, in 1755, close to forty Weymouth volunteers marched again under Captain Samuel Thaxter. This time, they marched all the way to Canada. One of the volunteers wrote back to a friend that the English regulars and the colonial volunteers had occupied Quebec and Montreal, and that French Generals Montcalm and Wolfe were defeated. New England had been saved from the French. The peace treaty was finally signed in Paris, France, in 1763. France gave up its rights to all of Canada to England. The French also gave up their rights to the lands and islands along the Saint Lawrence River and the disputed territory east of the Mississippi River down to, but not including, New Orleans. The king of England had more than doubled his claim in the New World."

"I guess that's the end of that story," said Tom, as he got up from the couch and headed for the cellar stairs.

"I don't think so. I think it's just the beginning of the story. The French have been driven back and have lost Canada. I'm sure the Indians helped the French because English settlers had taken—or forced them to sell—so much of their land earlier. Remember, Tom, the people in the colonies wanted to be free from the king of England. They didn't want to pay his taxes. They didn't want to lose their property, and they didn't really want to fight his wars! I think the trouble is just beginning. I'll see you tomorrow after school, and we'll find out," suggested Larry.

6

The next day, when the boys turned on the computer and monitor, the computer reported, "There had been very little rain the summer of 1762. There was a short growing season. The fishermen also did poorly because the waters off New England and the Cape had been overfished for many years. Men forgot about independence from England and worried more about feeding their families. That winter, many families had to borrow money in order to buy corn and flour. The next few years were hard years for almost everyone in New England. Some of the families moved back to Boston so that they could find work in the busier city. Other families moved to the South and the warmer climate or to the West, where large pieces of land could be claimed and settled. Some returned to Europe."

The computer voice continued, "Things returned to normal by 1768. Crops were good, and fish were plentiful again. Boston still needed lumber for building and firewood for her stoves and fireplaces. Europe needed fish for its dinner tables. The streets, shops, and wharves in Weymouth were busy again."

"Guess what I got on my history paper?" exclaimed Tom.

"I can imagine. I suppose you wrote about the Pilgrims or the Puritans or something like that and got an A."

"Why not? All I had to do was remember some of the great pictures that we saw on the monitor, especially those scenes in Charlestown, Boston, and Weymouth. Nothing to it," boasted Tom.

7

The next afternoon, when the boys activated the computer and the monitor again, they saw a picture of John Joy walking from his home toward the Landing. They saw him meet two men there. It was December 16, 1773. It was getting dark and cold.

"Is that you, John?" said Abraham Torrey softly.

"That's John, all right. Can't you tell by his walk?" said Jamy Nash, as the two men stepped out of the shadows to greet their friend. Jamy had been visiting the Torrey family. He had heard that something big was going to happen in Boston, and he wanted to be part of it.

"How are we going to get to Boston?" asked Abe.

"Are you coming with us, Jamy?" asked John.

"If you'll let me, I'd love to join you."

"Well, let's be off. I wouldn't miss Sam Adams for the world. That man is a real Patriot!" exclaimed John.

Larry and Tom watched the men walk down Commercial Street and heard Jamy ask, "What is this meeting at the old meetinghouse in Boston all about? What's the big secret?"

"If you are going to join us, you've got to be able to keep a secret. Can you do that?" asked John.

Jamy nodded his head. The three men walked on into the twilight.

John spoke, lifting one finger toward the sky. "First, our great great-grandparents came across the ocean to settle and secure this land for the king of England and make their dreams of freedom come true. Second, we helped his redcoats drive the French back into Canada to secure our northern New England borders. Then, our ungrateful king decides to order us to pay his redcoats' salaries—in gold, no less—for saving us from the French! *They* saved *us*? Wait a minute. *We* saved *them*, didn't we? If it weren't for the colonial volunteers, the redcoats would still be fighting and losing their scalps up there in the North Country. The gall of that man! Back in 1768, the king wanted us to take his soldiers into our homes and feed them, as well. I guess the final straw came when the people in Boston were asked to pay a tax on English tea. The captain of the ship apparently told the Bostonians that if they didn't pay the king's tea tax, the tea would remain aboard the ship and not be delivered to the company that ordered it. I understand that Sam Adams and John Hancock have protested and are refusing to pay the tax. You've heard of them, haven't you?"

"I understand that they are Boston bigwigs. I know that Sam Adams has spoken out against the king a number of times," replied Jamy.

"Anyway," John continued, "Adams, Hancock, and a silversmith by the name of Paul Revere have called a meeting of interested men from some of the surrounding towns. That meeting is tonight. That's where we're going!"

"I can't wait to hear what they've got to say and what they plan to do," exclaimed Abe Tower.

"What's all that got to do with us?"

"What happens in Boston can happen in Weymouth. Those are our friends up there. Some of them are our cousins. There's more and more talk about freedom from the king and from England. More and more men are talking about us becoming free colonies and writing all our own laws. I don't want the king's governors telling me what to do all the time. I don't want the king's soldiers watching over us all the time. I want to be free, completely free. I want my children to be free and grow up in a free society, a free country."

"Sounds like I've heard this story before," laughed Jamy. "Freedom to be a what?"

"Our own country—our own nation!" proclaimed John.

"This stuff about independence and patriotism confuses me. Are you a Patriot? You are one of them, aren't you? You're one of them too, aren't you, Abe? You're both Patriots!"

"A Patriot, I am," declared John proudly. "And Abe is, too!"

Larry and Tom watched John slap Abe on the back and say, "We'd better be off." The three men climbed into a wagon and headed for Boston.

Next, the monitor showed them among a large crowd of men, women, and children outside the old meetinghouse in Boston. The boys watched the crowd grow silent as the doors opened, and Sam Adams came out on the balcony to speak. They heard him say, "This meeting can do nothing more to save the country."

"Oh! Oh! That means trouble. Those are the passwords," reported John.

The computer reported, "A rumor spread through the crowd that the English governor, Hutchinson, and Sam Adams could not reach an agreement. The governor was not going to let the locally-owned ship leave the harbor if the tea tax was not paid."

The monitor showed a group of men, dressed like Indians, coming out of the back door of the meetinghouse and head down to the wharf, where the ship carrying the tea was tied up.

"Look, Indians!" exclaimed Jamy.

"I don't think so," answered Abe. "Those men are from the Masonic Lodge. I recognize two of them. They spoke at our Blue Lodge last month."

"They sure look like Indians. Where are they going?"

"Well, I'll be!" exclaimed John. "Are you with me, boys? Let's join in the fun. We'll show the king what we think of his tea and his tea tax!"

The crowd of men and cheering boys rushed down to the wharf. Tom and Larry watched while the men dressed as Mohawk and Narragansett Indians boarded the ship, held the crew at bay, opened the boxes of tea, and threw the tea into Boston Harbor.

"Jamy, what do you think about being a Patriot now?" asked Abe.

"Looks like fun to me!"

"It won't be fun for long. Believe me. Fighting for our freedom will not be fun at all. It'll be very dangerous. But we've got to do it. We've got to do it!" proclaimed John Joy.

The computer voice reported, "Later, a group of Patriots stormed the Bourne House in Marshfield and took all the English tea and burned it at a place they later called Tea Rock Hill."

Larry's mother called down from the kitchen. It was time for supper. Tom was going to stay at Larry's house for supper and a sleepover. His mother had to go away to visit her brother in the hospital.

"Just when it was getting exciting," said Tom.

"We don't have any homework tonight," said Larry. "We'll come back down and see what happens next. I think we are going to see the American Revolutionary War."

8

After the boys ate supper, they returned to the cellar playroom and the computer and monitor that had become such a part of their lives for the past few weeks. They touched the screen to turn the computer and monitor back on. The picture on the monitor showed the inside of a meetinghouse. Most of the men from Weymouth were at the meeting. The boys watched and listened as the elder Bates spoke out. "The day after Christmas, what a day to have a meeting."

"What's this all about?" asked Asa White as he and Thomas Nash entered the meetinghouse.

"Gentlemen, the trouble in Boston is getting worse," announced Cotton Tufts. "Since the parliament in England passed the Port of Boston Law, English ships have blockaded our port. No colonial ships can enter or leave the harbor. Our trade is being cut off. General Gage has come from New York to take command of the redcoats and has been ordered to take our guns and ammunition. I have word from the Correspondent's Committee in Dorchester that there could be trouble down here in Weymouth, too. I want a man to stand guard here at the meetinghouse and watch over the ammunition closet. Now is the time to be counted, gentlemen. We can't have the king's soldiers taking our guns and ammunition. We've got to stand up for our rights. We'll need men to stand guard around the clock. We'll need men on guard at the mouth of both rivers also. That way, we'll be ready in a minute if trouble comes our way. I understand that every town will be on guard. They are calling themselves Minutemen. Who'll volunteer?"

"I'll volunteer!" cried out Jesse Webb.

"I will also!" shouted Thomas Bicknell.

Tom and Larry watched as Cotton Tufts read the list of men and then explained, "That'll do it. That's enough for now. The rest of you will be called on later. We've got a town to protect. The meeting in Concord asked all the towns to stop paying taxes to the king's tax collector. We'll need all our money to buy more guns and ammunition if this thing goes the way it seems to be going."

"Do you think there's going to be a war?" asked Nathaniel Bayley.

9

The monitor showed a man riding on horseback into the village center in North Weymouth, where a crowd had gathered on April 19, 1775.

"That must be the courier. He's coming back from the meeting in Boston."

The boys watched as a young man dismounted from his sweaty horse and exclaimed, "The English troops marched toward Concord and Lexington and tried to capture John Hancock. Paul Revere and a friend of his rode to Lexington to warn them in time. They stopped the redcoats cold. The Minutemen stopped the English advance and sent them running! They hid behind trees and ambushed the redcoats as they marched in order down the road. They don't know how to fight our kind of war."

Tom and Larry heard the crowd cheer as the young Patriot continued, "Boston is full of redcoats. Hancock has called for all Patriots to join together to drive them out of New England. John Adams and the delegates of the Continental Congress in Philadelphia have asked George Washington to come up from Virginia to Boston and help organize an army." The boys watched as a teenager brought a fresh horse out of the stable and watched the courier mount and report, "I've got to ride on to Hingham and then on to Cohasset and Scituate to pass the word."

"They say Washington is a powerfully big man. If he is our commanding officer, we'll surely get help from the southern colonies, especially New Jersey, Virginia, and the Carolinas," predicted Doctor Tufts.

"What's the word from Sam Adams?" asked James Humphrey.

Doctor Tufts replied, "We'll hear from Dorchester tomorrow. But I expect that he'll ask all the towns to organize their men and send troops to join up somewhere near Boston. Washington will want to review the troops to see what he's got to work with. It is expected that he'll be in Boston by July 2."

"What's your read on this situation, Sol?" asked Nathaniel Bayley.

Larry and Tom watched as the crowd turned to their leader, Solomon Lovell. "I expect that the time has come, gentlemen. Cushing and Trufant, you two take charge. Gather the guns and the ammunition, and organize the men. The call to arms has come. If we are to be free from the king of England, we must be prepared to fight. I'm going to Boston. I'll be back with our orders."

The boys watched as a calm quietness came over the crowd. The realization of war had set in.

10

"I guess we are going to see the American Revolutionary War," said Tom.

"This is unbelievable. It's just like we are there. I can't believe it. We've got to let someone know about this computer. We can't keep this a secret much longer. This is something else. I wonder how they do it. Technology, technology. Wow!"

The boys watched the image on the monitor zoom in on Mrs. Tufts and Mrs. Howes. They were having tea with a group of women in the church hall in June, 1775. The women were exchanging stories about the events of the week. Mrs. Tufts was telling a story about a young lady from the town of Cohasset. "It seems that a colonial sailor came to her home to tell her that her husband had been taken from his ship by the English and that they had taken him and other prisoners to England!"

Mrs. Humphrey came into the room and interrupted. "Ladies, there was a brawl between some redcoats and some citizens in Boston. Abel Kent told me that Josh Bates was there right in the middle of it. I'm sorry, I didn't mean to interrupt," she finished.

"Did any of our boys get hurt?" asked Mrs. Howes.

"I haven't heard. All I know is that Washington is taking command of the troops and that he has sent a troop of men to New York to drag cannon back to Boston in order to better defend the harbor. He thinks that if we could put cannon on Dorchester Heights, aimed toward the harbor, we might sink some of those English ships out there, and they might retreat. But our main problem now is getting more guns and ammunition to defend Weymouth if and when the English troops decide to attack us. Our boys took most of the ammunition and guns with them when they marched off to Boston to sign up with General Washington."

The picture on the monitor focused on Mrs. Tufts, who returned to her story about Persis Lincoln in Cohasset. "I guess that Cohasset was having the same problem with ammunition and guns that we have. Anyway, the story goes that she got in a small dinghy and rowed across the bay to Gloucester at night, right under the noses of the British fleet, and returned with the ammunition and guns necessary to defend her town. It is said that she said that she would do anything to help end the war so that her husband could return home."

"Well, she sure did!" exclaimed Mrs. Howes. "She's a real heroine, a woman Patriot!"

11

When the boys activated the computer and monitor system on Sunday afternoon, they saw that a small crowd of men, women, and children had gathered. They were saying good-bye to the second troop of men called up for the war. Mrs. Beale waved good-bye to her husband and his friend Lot Witcomb, as the others marched out of town.

Mrs. Bates turned to Mrs. Pratt and lamented, "That's forty more of our men gone."

"We'll lose them all!" cried another woman as she turned her back and stomped up the dirt road.

"They'll be back. They'll all be back soon," Nellie Holbrook assured the others. "Now we've got work to do. We've got to make bread and corncakes to send to our men. They'll need good food and rations. They'll want warm clothes. Some of them will need bandages. We've got work to do!"

The boys watched as the women walked back toward their homes. They heard Mrs. Vinson tell Mrs. Joy, "I understand that General George Washington has a plan for getting the redcoats out of Boston and out of the area. I overheard Tom Nash tell Caleb Pratt that Washington plans to surprise the English in some way. Tom is working on General Washington's staff. He knows what's going on. He said something about the Dorchester Heights and cannon from Fort Ticonderoga. I didn't really hear the rest of the conversation. Tom closed the library door so I couldn't listen. I think he expects the cannon to be here by next March."

The monitor showed a picture of redcoats climbing up a hill in Boston and getting ready to attack a group of Patriots who had taken a position halfway up the hill to defend it. The computer narrated the scene. "On June 17, 1775, English troops decided to attack the town of Boston. The English had already taken over the harbor. The first real battle took place at Breed's Hill. General Putnam was outnumbered, 1500 colonial volunteers to 2600 redcoats. It was there, that day, that the Patriot general cried the famous orders: 'Don't shoot until you see the whites of their eyes!'"

Next, the monitor showed Abigail Adams, her young son, John Quincy Adams, and one of General Warren's young daughters, Abby, climbing Penn's Hill just south of the Adams's farm in Braintree. The computer explained, "Abigail Adams was babysitting the Warren children at the farm in Braintree. She could hear the noise of gunshots and ship's cannon off in the distance. Her husband, John, had warned her of the English attack on Boston. When she heard the distant gunfire, she took her son and General Warren's daughter with her and climbed Penn's Hill to observe the battle at Breed's Hill across the bay. They watched as the English troops defeated the Patriots that day. As the sounds of battle ceased, she returned to her house, only to learn a few hours later that General Warren had been killed. She had to break the news to his youngest daughter."

The monitor showed a high pile of round fieldstones standing at the top of Penn's Hill in Braintree. The computer voice narrated: "A pile of stones was later placed where Abigail Adams stood and watched the siege of Boston and the Battle of Breed's Hill. The pile is called a cairn, and it remains standing there to this day. Breed's Hill was named Bunker Hill after the war. John Knox a young Patriot, fought at Breed's Hill that day. Later, in December, 1775, he traveled to Fort Ticonderoga and brought the cannon from New York over the snow-covered trails to place it on Dorchester Heights in March, 1776."

The monitor showed the shoreline in North Weymouth on March 17, 1776. Hearing the ringing of the church bells, folks came running. "What's going on? What's happened?" asked an excited teenager. Another pointed past the islands out toward Boston Bay. They could see a fleet of ships far beyond, heading out to the harbor.

"They're leaving," Mrs. Litchfield yelled. "Look at them run!"

"I guess old Captain Webb's boys got after them redcoats after all!" exclaimed Henry Lambert, another town defender. "Those cannons on Dorchester Heights showed them we mean business. We may have lost the battle of Breed's Hill, but we won the battle of Boston Harbor!"

"It's the English navy! The English ships are leaving! The redcoats are on the run!" yelled another teenager. The children in the crowd gave a big cheer, and the women cried.

The computer reported, "The English navy moved out of the bay and anchored just outside of the harbor for close to three months, out of the range of the Dorchester Heights cannon. The English would not let colonial ships enter or leave the harbor. The blockade stopped trade and stymied the fishing fleet. Finally, cannon fire from Long Island in Boston Bay and from Hull Point to the south drove the English ships out of the bay and northward toward Nova Scotia with a number of local Loyalists aboard."

One woman announced, "Well, our men will be home soon, thank God."

The boys watched as the monitor's screen switched to an evening meeting where Cotton Tufts was talking. "The fighting isn't over. The English navy may have headed for Nova Scotia, but our colonial army is chasing the English army down the coast. They'll catch them in New York, New Jersey, or Delaware. But thank God, the fighting in Massachusetts is probably over. I think that this day, March 17, 1776, is the last day we have to worry about English troops coming to our houses, capturing our men, or taking our food and livestock."

The screen showed a group of neighbors and businessmen disagreeing over the war, taxes, and loyalty to the king. The computer explained, "There were citizens in every town who sided with the king of England. They were called Loyalists. They were not trusted or liked by their neighbors and by the Patriots who had fought for freedom and independence. Often, Loyalists and Patriots argued and got into fistfights or even barroom brawls. As the English army and navy left Boston and the surrounding towns, it was no longer safe for Loyalists to remain in New England. Many Loyalists moved to Nova Scotia, an English colony protected by English troops and the English navy. Much of Canada was still French, even though they lost the French and Indian War to England. But Nova Scotia was very Scottish, very English, and very safe for Loyalists who left New England and still supported the king of England."

The boys watched the monitor as family after family packed up and left for Nova Scotia by ship. The computer voice reported, "The descendants of the Billington family, who came over on the Mayflower and who had moved from Plymouth to Seekonk over one hundred years earlier, were Loyalists. They decided to move to Nova Scotia for their own safety. The Uthuessens, a Dutch family from New Amsterdam, New York, also moved to Nova Scotia at the same time for the same reasons. Thousands of Loyalists from New England and New York fled to Nova Scotia during and after the Revolutionary War."

"That's where one of my parents came from. I wonder if my ancestors were Loyalists?" questioned Larry.

"I've traced my grandparents and ancestors back to Ireland and to Italy," said Tom.

"We've got a project in history next month on genealogy. We're supposed to find out where our parents, grandparents, and great-grandparents came from."

"Yeah, I have already started working on mine. I've asked my mother," said Tom.

The boys shut off the computer. The monitor went black. They went up to the kitchen table and did their homework. Tom slept in the guest room.

12

The next afternoon, when the boys turned on the computer, it reported, "Patriot leaders from Massachusetts and the other twelve colonies were asked to travel to Philadelphia, Pennsylvania, for a second meeting to plan their next move. At that meeting of the Continental Congress, a Patriot from Virginia, Richard Henry Lee, made a passionate plea to continue the fight for independence. The citizens of Weymouth voted in June, 1776, to continue to support the colonial army. There was talk that the colonies up and down the Atlantic coast should unite and become an independent country, a new nation."

The boys watched and heard an old-timer sitting in Rice's Tavern in Commercial Square in the East Village say, "First we were an Indian village on the river with marshes, hay fields, and forests. Then, we were a small farming and fishing village, and now a town. I can see it now, the Commonwealth of Massachusetts. Who knows, someday we might even become a new nation! What will we call ourselves then? We've come a long way!"

"Thanks to our fathers and their fathers before them!" exclaimed another.

The boys heard the crowd cheer and one man yell out, "Amen to that!"

One Loyalist proclaimed, "We'll all die fighting for this thing you call freedom."

An old-timer replied, "You'd better join the rest of your Loyalist friends and head for Nova Scotia!" The crowd roared its approval.

Another asked, "What do you think will happen?"

Mr. Burrell, who had been listening to the discussion, answered, "We'll know soon enough. We'll know when Tom Jefferson, Ben Franklin, our old friend John Adams, and the others down in Philadelphia decide what to do next. I think we're going to claim independence, and then all hell will break loose. The king will not want us to be a free nation. He'll send more troops over here. This war may last for years!"

The picture on the monitor switched to a warm July day on the common in Philadelphia. The children were playing games, singing songs like "Yankee Doodle," and playing soldiers at war.

The picture quickly changed to a large meeting hall. The boys watched as John Hancock motioned to Ben Franklin. "Ben, may I see you for a minute?" John Hancock walked across the large hall and said to Ben Franklin, "We have only two days before the vote. I'm not sure that all the representatives here agree with Henry Lee. We've got to come up with an idea to convince them. We've got to convince them all that freedom and independence from England is our only answer. Ben, we need something different. We need something strong. We need something that will move the people and show our strong feelings about this matter."

"You mean something like Patrick Henry would say? A strong proclamation like 'Give me liberty or give me death!'"

The boys watched, as both men laughed and nodded their heads in agreement.

"Well, we do need something with a little fire in it. We need to be unanimous on this," declared Hancock, as he looked over to a table where three men sat talking quietly.

Ben Franklin pointed to the three men and said, "I thought Tom Jefferson and old John Adams over there were working on that. Is that Livingston with them?"

John Hancock replied, "They are, Ben. But I want you to work with them. You're a man of letters. You've traveled to Europe. You've felt the wave of revolution over there, in France and elsewhere. You have the background to help them come up with the words we need to stir up the people so that the king will see that there is no choice for him but to leave New England and the southern colonies. You have skills and experience in diplomacy. He's got to understand that we want him to pull his redcoats out, forever!"

"And, if not, John?" asked Ben Franklin in a somber voice.

"If not, then for sure our declaration has got to be written so well and so strongly that the words will inspire every single colonist to fight to the end for the cause of freedom and independence. Ben, tell me one thing in life that is more fundamental and more important than personal freedom!"

"Dry feet and a warm stove," laughed Ben. "You know I'm only kidding," added old Ben Franklin.

"I know, Ben, you like to kid a lot. But you are a famous scientist and inventor, a successful diplomat. Your writings and your newspaper are highly respected, especially your Poor Richard's Almanac. You are a man of letters. We need your wisdom. Jefferson will benefit from your discussions. He is a talented writer as well."

John Hancock took Ben Franklin by the arm and led him across the room to where the men were sitting.

"Gentlemen, I've asked Ben to work with you. He has a very good background in politics. He has spoken with ambassadors and kings alike. I think he can help."

"Well, gentlemen, if I can't help, I'll give you a few laughs!" chuckled Ben as he pulled up a chair to join the men at the table. Then Ben Franklin grew serious. "Let's see where we are. Let's see where we're going."

The boys watched John Hancock turn on his heel and begin to walk away. He looked back over his shoulder and said, "Gentlemen, I pray that you inspire us all with your language and declaration."

The computer voice reported, "On July 2, 1776, the colonial leaders, meeting in Philadelphia, declared their independence from the king of England. Thomas Jefferson, with the help of Ben Franklin, wrote most of what became known as the Declaration of Independence."

"I think that Ben Franklin may have been our greatest American of all time. I read his biography. The guy was brilliant. He invented so many things like the wood-burning stove. He started the postal service and wrote the almanac. He started the public library. His experiments with static electricity opened the door to an understanding of how current electricity works and how it can be used. He represented the colonies and then the United States in England and France as our ambassador. The guy was a genius, I tell you," proclaimed Larry.

13

When Larry and Tom returned to the computer the next afternoon, the picture on the monitor showed Reverend Smith in front of a crowd outside the First Church. It was August 11, 1776. Folks gathered around. He began to read. "When in the course of human events it becomes necessary …"

"Never mind reading all those fancy words," said one old man. "Just tell us what it all means."

The folks watched as the Reverend read the paper silently and then spoke out. "It's a letter to the king. It's a declaration. It says that all men are created equal, and that God gave all men the right to be free."

"Amen!" cried the crowd.

Reverend Smith went on, "It says that people have the right to choose their own leaders and that the leaders should be elected by the people. The letter says that the king has not let us make our own laws and that he has sent soldiers to our towns to collect taxes from us. It says that he told his redcoats that they could live in our homes. It says that he has stopped our ships from sailing and has tried to cut off our trade with other countries. It says his governors punish our people without a trial and a jury. It says that he has taken away our charter."

"I didn't know he took away our charter. That's our land. He can't claim it back!" cried out one old-timer.

"Go on, keep on talking," urged another.

Larry and Tom watched as the crowd inched closer. "It says that his soldiers have burned our towns and killed our people and that he has kidnapped our sailors. It says that the colonies declare that they are free and will fight to keep this freedom with our lives and our honor."

"That does mean a long war!" proclaimed one woman.

"Look, Adams signed it," reported the traveling cobbler.

"If Adams signed it, then it's good enough for me," remarked another Patriot, as he clutched his long gun.

The boys listened as one woman said, "General Washington will want more of our men now. When will this ever end?"

"Is freedom worth all this?" asked another mother.

"Freedom is worth everything!" exclaimed storekeeper Torrey.

14

The picture on the monitor moved to a tent on the Pennsylvania side of the Delaware River where General George Washington and his officers were looking over maps and making plans for a Christmas Eve surprise.

The computer voice explained, "After the English navy and army left Boston in March and while the women of Weymouth were making warm clothes and bandages to send to their men on Christmas Eve, 1776, George Washington and his officers were planning a surprise attack against the English and the German mercenaries called Hessians on the other side of the Delaware River in Trenton, New Jersey. They hoped the attack would bring the war to a quick end. The colonial army had just retreated across the Delaware River from New Jersey into Pennsylvania. The redcoats were convinced that the colonists were on the run. The English soldiers and their German allies drank and ate heavily on Christmas Eve to celebrate what they thought was victory after the colonial retreat. That night, at midnight, in the dark, and through the icy waters, Washington's troops crossed back over the Delaware River in small boats and marched back into New Jersey."

The boys watched the scene on the monitor, which showed Washington's six thousand troops surprising and capturing the English and German soldiers at Trenton.

The computer voice continued, "News of Washington's victory on December 26, 1776, at Trenton, was a good Christmas present for the families back home. Another victory, as Saratoga was recaptured, convinced the colonial leaders that they could defeat the redcoats. One colonial soldier wrote home from Valley Forge, where the colonial troops trained and camped for the cold, bitter winter, 'The victory at Saratoga is the turning point of the war. I am sure that the war will be over soon, and the king's army and navy will be forced to return to England. We will be free and independent.'"

"I saw a movie on TV about the surprise attack at Trenton. There is a famous painting that shows George Washington standing at the front of a boat crossing the Delaware River on Christmas Eve. He surprised them, all right," reflected Tom.

"Boy, time sure flies when we're watching this thing. It makes you feel like you're right there," Larry commented.

Larry shut down the computer and monitor. "I think this story is almost over. Remember, the title was *Independence Won*," said Tom, as they walked up the cellar stairs.

15

That Saturday morning, when the boys turned the computer and monitor on again, the monitor showed a group of teenagers talking at the general store in the South Village.

"I wish I were old enough to vote. Our laws are fine, but I can't understand why I can't vote next week. I can go off and fight the redcoats, but I can't vote! That doesn't seem right to me," complained one of the young men.

"Who would you vote for if you could vote for governor?" asked his friend.

"I'd vote for Ben Lincoln, from Hingham. I think he'd make a great governor."

"My father says that the Massachusetts state Constitution reads a little like the Declaration of Independence," added another teenager.

"Well, Hancock helped write that too, remember? I think that John Hancock should be our first elected governor. How can General Lincoln be governor? He's still down around Yorktown somewhere with Colonel Nathanial Greene, finishing off the redcoats," argued one of the boys standing nearby.

"I think the war is almost over. I understand that the English are surrounded at Yorktown."

"No matter who is elected governor here in Massachusetts, we've got good and fair laws. Our new state constitution is well written. It says that all men are created equal and that no man in Massachusetts can be the owner of another. They'll be no slavery in this state! I think that's a good law," remarked one of the black teenagers in the crowd.

"I still think that if a man can go off and fight the war, he ought to be able to vote," argued another.

"Well, if Hancock is elected, I'll speak to him about that," laughed one of the teenagers. "He's a friend of the family."

"Sure, I know, he ships all that rum from the Caribbean into Boston and into your father's store. He and Hancock are millionaires!"

"He's a smart businessman is what he is."

Larry and Tom listened as the computer voice interrupted: "In 1780, the people of Massachusetts accepted the state constitution and elected their first governor and the first General Court under the new constitution, which was written mainly by John Adams, Sam Adams, and James Bowdoin. John Hancock was elected governor, and Ben Lincoln was elected lieutenant governor. James Humphrey was elected to represent Weymouth in the new state convention. Massachusetts was a free state, and the Revolutionary War was close to an end when the last of Weymouth's young men were called up to serve in the colonial army. In late October, 1783, word came that the war had ended. The redcoats had surrendered."

The boys watched as the monitor showed the English general surrendering his sword to the colonial general. The English troops stood at attention and then laid their guns down on the ground in front of them.

The boys listened to the computer. "The soldiers who came home told how Washington, the Swamp Fox, Dan Morgan, and General Greene from Rhode Island surrounded General Cornwallis and the English army at Yorktown. They described how the English tried to escape by sea and how DeGrasse's French ships blocked them and forced them back toward land and Washington's troops. On October 19, 1781, the war ended, as the redcoats laid down their guns in a solemn ceremony that English General Cornwallis did not attend. He left the area earlier for fear of his life. The thirteen colonies had won their freedom."

"Well, the war is over. Independence has been won. I guess that's the end of this story. What will we study next?" asked Tom.

"I'm not so sure this story is over," said Larry. "Come on over after school on Monday, and we'll find out."

16

When the boys activated the computer Monday after school, they saw two teenage boys hiding in the stables next to the First Church. The computer voice explained, "It was the spring of 1809. The Revolutionary War had been over for more than twenty years."

"Wow, that was quick!" exclaimed Tom.

"That's technology for you," replied Larry.

Larry and Tom saw the two teenagers crouched down behind a haystack in the stable next to the First Church

"Be quiet, Butch. The Reverend will hear us and come out and box our ears," whispered Junior.

"I hope we catch some herring," said Butch. "I'd hate to get paddled for nothing. I just know that we are going to get caught!"

"You worry too much," admonished Junior.

"Here, put my quill up there on the beam. If we break these new goose quills, the schoolmaster will have a fit," laughed Butch.

"Yes, and my mother will tar and feather me!" said Junior in a serious voice. "Here, put my Bible up there, too."

"Why did you bring your Bible?" asked Butch.

"I don't want my mother thinking all day long about why I left my Bible at home," answered Junior. "She would bring it to school and find me missing!"

"Good thinking. I wish I had thought of that," said Butch with a worried look on his face. "I left mine on my bed. Come on. Let's sneak on up to the brook. I never did like this idea of going to school until June. Who thought it up, anyway?"

"Yeah, my father told me that he went to school only a few months of the year. They had to work on the farm—especially at harvest time in September and October and then again during the planting season in April and May. They worked all summer," said Junior. "Boy, those olden days must have been great! Not so many months of school, that's for sure!"

"Where did you get those new boots?" asked Butch.

"My father bought them in the square. No more traveling cobblers for us. These were made at the new Tirrell shoe factory up on Front Street. One boot is made for the left foot and the other for the right one. There will be no more one shoe fits both feet. He said that the selectmen have approved plans for a couple more shoe factories in town. My uncle hopes to get a job in one of them," reported Junior.

The picture on the monitor showed the boys walking up and over King Oak Hill through the blueberry and apple tree fields beyond Commercial Street, where Memorial Field is today, toward Commercial Square, now called Jackson Square, and the Herring Run. Larry and Tom watched as Butch broke a branch off a nearby tree and took a small ball of string out of his pocket. They watched both boys make their own fishing poles.

"Look, he's hooked one already," reported Tom.

Larry and Tom listened as the young fishermen talked. "This is the life," reflected Butch. "I just hope we don't get caught. We missed that test on the United States Constitution today."

"That's why I wanted to skip school," admitted Junior. "I just don't understand what that's all about. And I really haven't studied much. You love history, Butch. I bet you know all about it. Tell me. Tell me about the Constitution. I'd rather know more about inventions and science, but tell me about the Constitution. You know I hate to read and write and all that stuff!"

"You remember when the schoolmaster told us about the Revolutionary War?"

"You mean when he talked about how some of the folks were in favor of the king instead of being on the side of the Patriots?" asked Junior.

"Yes, that's when some of the families left and went to Nova Scotia or back to England to live. Do you remember when the schoolmaster told us how the redcoats surrendered at Yorktown? Do you remember when he told us how the people of Massachusetts elected John Hancock as governor?"

"I remember that," responded Junior. "That's when all thirteen colonies, including Massachusetts, became states, like New York, Virginia, and so on. Oh shucks, I forget them all!"

"That's right. Remember how the schoolmaster told us that the laws of Massachusetts said that slavery was wrong and that no man could own another man and keep him as a slave and make him work? Do you remember the day that he told us about the different states and how they got into arguments because they had different laws?"

"I remember that day. That's the day I lost the spelling bee on the first word. I remember that he said the law in Massachusetts didn't allow slavery but that the law in Virginia did."

"That's right," answered Butch. See, you know more than you think you know. Now, let's get back to the United States Constitution. Well, with all the states arguing about slaves, business rules, voting, and taxes, and other things, it was decided that the states needed one set of laws that all the people in all the states would live by so that we would be united. That's what our grandfathers fought for. These laws are called the laws of the United States

Constitution. You see, we have local laws that we have to live by here in Weymouth, like who can be elected and how much tax we have to pay to run the town. Our selectmen and town meeting members make laws that we have to live by here in Weymouth. We also have state laws here in Massachusetts that all of us in Massachusetts have to live by, and we have the laws of the United States Constitution that everyone in every state and in every town has to live by and obey."

"We have three sets of laws? Why three sets?" asked Junior.

"We've got to have laws here in Weymouth just for us," explained Butch. "Special laws just for our town. We need laws here that tell us where we can build a house, where a blacksmith shop can be built, how many shoe factories can be built, or how much tax our fathers have to pay to the town to paint the town hall, put new stone on the roads, pay the schoolmaster's salary, and all those things. These are called town laws. We elect selectmen every couple years to help run our town. The people of the town meet at a town meeting every year and vote on what laws should be made and how the money collected from taxes and fees should be spent. Most historians, especially those who study Weymouth history, say that our Weymouth town meeting was the first town meeting ever held in Massachusetts. I think it was around 1641. That's over a hundred and fifty years ago. My mother told me that my great, great, great, great-grandfather was there. We also have to have laws for all the people who live in Massachusetts, too," continued Butch.

"But if each town has laws, why do we have to have state laws, Massachusetts laws?" asked Junior.

"Junior, the laws of one town may not be the same as the laws of another town. Some towns allow alcohol; others don't. Some towns have tolls on their roads; others don't. Different towns have different laws. That's okay. But everybody in all the towns has to obey the Massachusetts state laws."

"So we have to live by the laws passed here in Weymouth by our leaders at town meeting, and we also have to live by the laws passed in Boston by the Great and General Court and the governor. I get it," said Junior.

"Then there are the laws passed by the senators and representatives in Congress and signed by the President of the United States," added Butch.

"I get it! The United States Constitution is a set of laws for all the people of all the United States—all the people in every state and all the people in every town," said Junior proudly.

"That's right, the United States Constitution gives all the people in the United States the same rights and freedoms and the same laws to obey. That's important. The Constitution gives us the freedom that our ancestors fought for in 1776. The United States Constitution and the Bill of Rights give us our rights and our freedoms.

"The Constitution gives us the right to write whatever we want in the newspaper, as long as it's the truth. It gives us the right to have meetings and to say whatever we want, as long as we don't create bedlam or a riot. It gives us the right to go to any church we wish. It explains how the president and the Congress are elected and how you can even be elected president."

"Me, president? I doubt that," interrupted Junior.

Butch continued, "It explains how the president works with the other parts of the federal government. It explains the responsibilities of the different parts of the United States government and how they are supposed to work together to run our country. It explains how our senators and representatives make laws. It explains how judges and courts make sure everyone follows the law. One of the most important rights that the Constitution gives us all is a right to have a trial by a jury of our peers if we are accused by someone of breaking a law in the town, in the state, or in our country."

"You mean even I can be in the government?" asked Junior.

"That's right. If you could get enough people to vote for you, you could be in the local town government, the state government, or in the federal government. That's probably the greatest thing about the United States Constitution. The Constitution says that the people elect their own leaders. No one can take over the government, make laws, or change laws unless they have been elected. They usually must be in the majority to make laws. That's a good law. I think that the biggest reasons the colonies fought against the king, back in 1776, are that he took their property, made them pay unfair taxes, and wouldn't let the people pick their own leaders and make their own laws," added Butch.

Larry and Tom watched as the image on the monitor switched to a small schoolroom in the new school building. They listened as the schoolmaster questioned Junior and Butch. "Where were you two boys yesterday?"

"I was sick, sir, but I know all about the Constitution," said Junior.

"Good," said the schoolmaster. "Here is a copy of it. You can sit down over there and make two more copies of it for me!"

Junior glanced over at Butch as he headed for the far end of the room to carry out his punishment.

"Yes, and you too, Butch," said the schoolmaster. "You both had a fine day fishing yesterday. Now you can do twice as much work today. I'll see you boys in the woodshed after classes as well. After the strap, you can cut some wood. You see, there are the United States laws based on the United States Constitution and the laws passed by the United States senators and representatives in Congress each year and signed by the president. There are also the Massachusetts laws based on the Massachusetts state Constitution and those passed by the Massachusetts House of Representatives and Senate and signed by the governor each year. There are the laws and rules of our town passed by our town meeting members and our selectmen each year. Gentlemen, there are also the laws and rules of this school and my classroom. You have to obey them all!"

"And Ma's and Pa's laws and rules when I get home," Junior moaned to himself.

Larry and Tom watched the computer monitor fade into darkness.

"I guess that's the end of that story," said Tom.

"I expect so. We did learn about the birth of our town, the Revolutionary War, the birth of our state, and the birth of our nation. We don't have town meetings any more here in Weymouth. We have a mayor and town councilors who make the laws now. Time has changed things. I guess we should bring the computer and monitor back to the library now."

Tom interrupted, "No, let's keep it longer. I know it has lots more history to teach. Maybe it has some science to teach us, too. Maybe it could teach us about inventions. Wouldn't that be great! Please, Larry, let's keep it for a little while longer?"

"You haven't told anyone about this, have you?"

"No."

17

Just then the monitor came back on. The boys were surprised. They could see that the images on the screen were looking down from above. They could see buildings, cars, and, people below traveling through the busy centers of the four villages in town: Bicknell Square in North Weymouth, Weymouth Landing, Upper and Lower Commercial Square, which is often called Jackson Square, in East Weymouth, and Columbian Square in South Weymouth. The computer voice reported, "Today, there are over fifty thousand people living in Weymouth. There are three bridges in town. One still connects Braintree and Weymouth, where the Monataquot River and the Fore River meet in Weymouth Landing. A new bridge is being built over the Fore River where the old bridge connects North Weymouth and Quincy. A third bridge connects North Weymouth from Bridge Street to Hingham."

"Wow! This is some computer! Now we're up in a helicopter? Look, Tom, down there. There's where the old shipyard used to be. My dad told me that his dad worked there in the 1940s and helped build ships that fought in World War II."

"Looks like they're tearing it down. Why are those hundreds of cars parked down there?" asked Tom.

"I think that they are being stored there so that they can be sold by the automobile dealer over on Quincy Avenue," replied Larry. "There's the old Bicknell School. My dad says that there used to be over twenty schools in Weymouth in the 1970s and 1980s, when there were over twelve thousand kids in town. Now there are only seven thousand students, I think. A lot of the schools were closed down. Bicknell was sold by the town and made into condominiums."

The computer voice continued as the helicopter flew over North Weymouth. "Great Hill, a drumlin created by the glacier, remains today as it overlooks the Wessagusset Beach and reminds us of Indian life over five hundred years ago.

"Gristmills were built by the early settlers to grind corn into grain and cornmeal. They were usually built on rivers, where running and rushing waters could turn the water wheel, which turned a large, flat stone around and around on top of another flat stone to grind kernels of corn into grain. One of the first gristmills was built down there on the Fore River.

That area was called Mill Cove. The Massachuset Indians had a small village there. Today it's a boatyard."

"I know that boatyard! See, it's on the other side of the street, just before you get to the Johnson School down there," said Tom, pointing.

The computer continued, "Other mills that sawed logs into boards and ground corn were built on the river as it flowed down from Great Pond in South Weymouth to Mill Pond, which used to be on Mill Street in South Weymouth. It flowed down where the expressway is today, on to Whitman's Pond, to the Herring Run in East Weymouth, and out to the Back River in North Weymouth."

"There's the Abigail Adams House down there!" exclaimed Tom.

The computer reported, "The first school in Weymouth was built in 1681 on Church Street, right next to First Church, which you see down there. That church was built in 1833, after a fire destroyed the one built there in 1682.

"The Abigail Adams House today sits on Norton Street, at the foot of the Old North Cemetery. It was moved from Ford's farm off Sea Street, near the corner of Route 3A, in North Weymouth in 1947 by the Abigail Adams Society, which maintains the house today as an historical site. The North Cemetery down there was called Watch Hill and is where the first settlers built their first meetinghouse in 1623 and where they rebuilt it in 1641 because it was falling down. The first town meeting was held in the new meetinghouse there that year. A memorial stone to honor the Weymouth men who fought and died in the war between the North and the South in the 1860s was placed at the top of Watch Hill in 1868. The cannons were placed there in 1898. That cemetery is thought to be the first official cemetery in Weymouth."

The helicopter flew up and over King Oak Hill. The computer voice pointed out, "That mansion, on top of the hill and behind the trees, was built in 1904 and is an exact copy of George Washington's mansion, called Mount Vernon, which is located in Virginia.

"You will note that many streets in North Weymouth have Indian names. That's because North Weymouth is the oldest section of the town. When the main roads throughout the town were repaired and modernized during the late 1800s and early 1900s, trolley cars powered by overhead electric wires traveled on tracks from one section of the town to another and from Weymouth to Braintree and to Quincy. There were trolley tracks on Sea Street, North Street, Broad Street, Commercial Street, Pleasant Street, and Front Street, among others. They all lead from one end of town to the other."

The helicopter made a turn back over Watch Hill and toward the water and Great Hill. The computer explained, "When the foundation was dug for the house down there at 236 Sea Street, two headless skeletons were found in the ground. They are believed to belong to Witawaumet and Pecksuot, the two Indian chiefs who threatened those first settlers at Wessagusset. Remember, it was Miles Standish and his men who came up from Plymouth to save the members of Weston's first small trading company from an Indian attack there."

The helicopter flew over 43 Bicknell Road. "This is where seven skeletons and a number of colonial artifacts were found in a tomb in the ground when that house was built. They are believed to be the skeletons of some of Weston's men, the first settlers in North Weymouth. When the house was built, it is believed that five of the skeleton skulls were placed in the stone foundation."

The monitor continued to show pictures from the helicopter of Webb Park and the Great Esker Park, and the computer reported, "These areas have been preserved to protect the natural environment. The story of our Earth over time can be found and seen in the rocks, ledges, fields, and streams down there.

"There are a number of small islands off the North Weymouth shore. Grape Island was the scene of Weymouth's only battle with the redcoats during the American Revolution. A Mr. Leavitt owned the island and was loyal to the king, and allowed the English troops to use the hay on his island for their horses. When the English troops came by boat to load the hay and take it back to the Boston shore where they were camped, Minutemen on the shores of North Weymouth and neighboring Hingham rang church bells and sounded the alarm. The Patriot militias from both towns attacked the redcoats, drove them off the island, and set the island hay on fire. The episode has been called 'The Grape Island Alarm' by historians."

"Mr. Clarke from the Historical Society told me that story, too," commented Larry.

The boys watched and listened.

The monitor continued to show scenes of present-day Weymouth, as the helicopter flew toward East Weymouth. The computer voice explained, "The Herring Run in Jackson Square in East Weymouth still connects Whitman's Pond with the Back River. The ironworks on Iron Hill Street, next to the water ladder where the herring struggle to get up to the pond and have their babies, made nails and other iron materials in the early 1800s. One of the stone buildings remains there today."

The screen showed an old school building, and the computer explained, "The old Washington School is still there in Jackson Square. It was built in 1888. There were over fifty students in each of the four rooms. Each room had two grades. It was sold to an engineering company when it was closed.

"Peck's funeral home down there on Commercial Street used to be the Rice Tavern, where leaders of the town often met to discuss plans before and after town meetings in the mid- and late-1700s.

The town hall on Middle Street is a copy of the Old State House in Boston, where the leaders of the American Revolution often met. Next to the town hall is the Memorial Wall, where most of the men and woman who fought in the different wars over the years are memorialized. Their names appear on brass plates attached to the brick wall."

"My grandfather's name is there on the Memorial Wall. He was in the Korean War," noted Larry.

The computer reported, "There are schools named after each of the five Medal of Honor recipients in Weymouth. They are the Elden H. Johnson School, the Frederick C. Murphy School, the Lawrence W. Pingree School, the William Seach School, and the Ralph Talbot School. Those men are Weymouth heroes. Weymouth is believed to be the only town in the country with five Medal of Honor recipients. Over on Commercial Street you can see the Maria Weston Chapman Middle School. It used to be North High School. It was named after her because of the work she did in the middle 1800s to speak out and fight against slavery in our country. Her ancestors date back to the original but failed settlers in Weymouth led by Thomas Weston. The stone building on the right, just before the corner of Pleasant and Lake Streets, and across from the old police station, which is now a teen center, is named the Franklin Pratt Library. It sits on a piece of land that Franklin Pratt donated to the town. He ran a print shop there and was a Boy Scout leader in Weymouth for thirty years."

The helicopter banked a right and headed west. The computer explained, "If you drive up Broad Street through Central Square and head down that road, you'll come to the present-day Electro Switch Company down there on the left. Before that building was built, the Hunt family made fireworks there beginning in the middle 1800s.

"Up the street into Lincoln Square, just up the hill from Weymouth Landing, there is a stone fire station that is closed. There have been three stations on that site over the years. Two of them burned down in 1872 and 1929. They finally built a stone fire station there. The town has closed some old fire stations and has built new ones in the last ten or fifteen years or so. The first fire stations were just one-room buildings where the fire wagon was kept. Some of those buildings are still standing. There's one in Lovell's Corner and another on Front Street, just past the Stetson Shoe Building. The VFW Hall on Broad Street, back in East Weymouth, used to be a fire station, too. The horses usually grazed in hay fields near the stations. Horses grazed at Mitchell's Field next to the present-day Abigail Adams School on Middle Street. The horses were trained to leave the field and gallop down the streets to the station when they heard the fire bell ringing. Then they were hooked up to the fire wagon and galloped off to the fire. Children scampered to their backyards for safety."

The monitor showed the Tufts Library, and the computer voice spoke. "The library was named after the Tufts family, who played a major role in the story of Weymouth. They lived in that large house at 246 Commercial Street, just past where the Arnold Tavern once stood and where the men, including Cotton Tufts, met to plan the defense of the town during the French and Indian War and during the American Revolution. The tavern was built in 1741. It was later replaced by a movie theater and a block of stores in 1927. It looks like an empty lot today."

"There's the Tufts Library," pointed out Larry. "That's where we got this computer. There's a history museum downstairs there. It's run by volunteers from the Weymouth Historical Society. They've got lots of stuff from the past on display there. There's an old dugout canoe there that was found at Great Pond in South Weymouth. I know that Indians lived in North

Weymouth, but I bet there was an Indian camp on the shores of the Great Pond, too. I like to read the articles in the *Weymouth News* that Theodore G. Clarke writes about Weymouth's history. He's chairperson of the town's Historical Commission. He wrote a great book about Weymouth's history," finished Larry, as he pointed to the Tufts Library, as if he expected the computer to talk back to him. It did.

The computer reported, "The original Tufts Library was built in 1891 next to the site of the present Sacred Heart Church in the Landing. It was torn down in 1966 to help make the roads wider in Weymouth Landing Square and to move to a new library building built in Lincoln Square on Broad Street, across from the old Hunt School, which is now a Christian Academy."

As the helicopter flew over Weymouth Landing, Larry exclaimed, "There's the new Sacred Heart Church. It was just recently built after a fire destroyed the original one a few years ago."

The monitor showed cars traveling up Front Street out of the Landing and onto Summer Street. The computer reported, "Here on Summer Street and Front Street were some of the early, large farms in the middle 1600s,,1700s, and 1800s. You can see the fieldstone walls that separated family farms, which have been there for over 250 years. This is also where much of the logging took place. The logs were carted down to the Landing at the docks. Logs were shaped into lumber at the saw mill and the lumberyard there on the Fore River and shipped to Boston and to England. The lumberyard that was there on the river on Commercial Street is gone, as are so many other historic buildings, which have been torn down over time."

The helicopter tour took the boys to South Weymouth. "There's the old Stetson shoe factory," explained Larry. "My dad said that it was one the biggest shoe factories in town. Hundreds of people worked there. It closed in 1973. The building is mostly full of doctor's offices now. I read that the first shoe factory was built by James Terrill on Front Street and that a pair of shoes cost between two and three dollars back then, in 1808. Dad said that there were shoe factories all over town in the 1800s and early 1900s. My grandfather told me that there was a big one in Columbian Square, South Weymouth, at the corner of Union and Pleasant streets. That building is still there. He said that there were others on Charles Street, on Middle Street back in East Weymouth, and on Sea Street in North Weymouth."

The computer voice reported as the helicopter flew over South Weymouth, "That big stone building down there is the Fogg Building. It was called the 'Opera House' when it was built in 1888 by the Fogg family. It's an apartment house now. The stone building across the street is the Fogg Library. It was the first library in Weymouth. You can see that its exterior walls are being repaired. The Community Preservation Committee in town is helping pay for the project. There is a memorial stone there in front of the library dedicated to the men who lost their lives in World War II.

"Across the street from the Saint Francis Xavier Church was the site of the first Catholic church in Weymouth. There's a parking lot there now. The church was destroyed by fire in

1869 and rebuilt where it stands now, along with a number of new Catholic churches in town, including the Immaculate Conception Church in 1873. The modern church you see down there now was built in 1967. It is still named after Saint Francis Xavier."

"There's the Holbrook house on Ralph Talbot Street. The Weymouth Historical Society has a museum in that old house," observed Tom.

The computer explained, "That large and expanding building project you see down there at the corner of Columbian Street and Route 18 is the South Shore Hospital complex. The hospital started in the Reed home there in 1922.

"Patients come from all over the South Shore to receive health care there today.

"Over there on Pond Street are the railroad tracks where the first railroad came through Weymouth from Abington in 1845.

"Now you can see the South Weymouth Naval Air Station. It was a very active air base over the years and played a major role in guarding our east coast during recent wars. It's closed now."

"That must have been a big air base. Look, you can see the new roads going in there now. My dad says that they are going to build hundreds of new homes and businesses in there," Larry commented.

"And a new golf course, too," added Tom.

The boys watched the monitor as the helicopter came down on the old landing area at the base. The computer concluded, "You have seen and heard the story of Weymouth from its geological beginnings up to and including the Revolutionary War when it became part of the United States of America. You have had a lesson in government. You have just visited some of the historical places in town that our story mentioned. I hope you can return sometime to see and hear about some other topic that might interest you. Until then, good-bye and keep reading and keep on learning."

The monitor went blank, and the computer voice went silent.

"Can you keep this a secret?" asked Larry.

"I hope so," answered Tom.

"Tom, what do you want to be when you grow up?"

"I want to be a helicopter pilot, you?"

"I want to be a history teacher," concluded Larry.